A CHAT OVER COFFEE

BY

JEAN HAMLYN

authorHOUSE®

AuthorHouse™ UK Ltd.
500 Avebury Boulevard
Central Milton Keynes, MK9 2BE
www.authorhouse.co.uk
Phone: 08001974150

© 2009 Jean Hamlyn. All rights reserved.

No part of this book may be reproduced, stored in a retrieval system, or transmitted by any means without the written permission of the author.

First published by AuthorHouse 10/1/2009

ISBN: 978-1-4389-9169-6 (sc)

This book is printed on acid-free paper.

DEDICATION

This is a dedication to my daughters and friends, and those who just love to do 'coffee or lunch'. It's so nice to have time for a chat, people are in such a hurry these days and time goes by so quickly. My girls are always texting, or on their mobile phones, and a conversation is virtually impossible without the interruption of the phone, or children, wanting something whilst you are trying to talk. So sit down, make a cup of coffee and have a chat with me in this book. You owe it to yourself for a little quiet time, if you fall asleep all well and good, it won't hurt. What is it we are all rushing around for anyway?

When looking in the mirror and seeing a face that is not familiar, I wonder where time has gone. Although I have been married to Mike for a few years now, it seems like only yesterday when I was a young woman on my own bringing up my girls after a divorce. Taking them to the childminder; then going on to work, collecting them on my way home, cooking dinner, washing, shopping, ironing and cleaning and making clothes for them. Taking them to dancing, brownies, guides, band etc how did I have the time? I know - I didn't have a computer then.

CONTENTS

Dedication
1. Two Coffees Please
2. Mine Or Yours
3. A Passion At My Feet
4. Glittery Things
5. Vacuum Sealed
6. Teacake Anyone?
7. If I Can Remember
8. Night School
9. Too Much Or Not Enough
10. One In The Eye
11. Have I Been There Already?
12. A Change In Shape
13. Sun Cream, Or Sun Burn?
14. Monty Versus Ted
15. Crimpers
16. Memories

Chapter 1

TWO COFFEES PLEASE

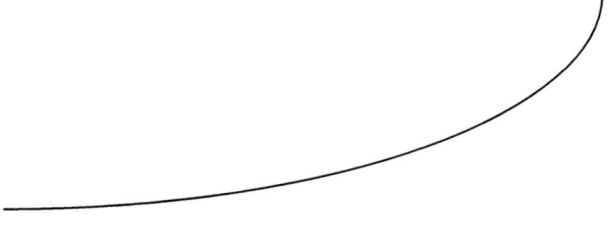

'Once upon a time' doesn't that phrase take you back to childhood and all the stories you heard at your mother's knee, or when you were snuggled up in bed with her beside you reading a favourite story. I often think of my mother who so loved reading. She was always buying us books and taking us to the local library when we were youngsters. At Christmas there would always be an annual in my stocking, or one for my birthday.

So I have my mother to thank for getting me into reading.

My brother Peter and I would walk across fields and hills to our local library, it was deemed a safer way to go, rather than walking along a roadway. But doubt I would go through fields for miles to a library today, especially when you had to carry books back with you. If they hadn't been returned before the allotted time, a reminder card would come through the letterbox and a fee had to be paid (usually out of our pocket money). We would be told off if we forgot to take the books back on time and would always get a scowl from the Librarian as she stamped the book. It was a Saturday morning trip that we children usually looked forward to and we so loved looking through the rows and rows of books.

The thing is with a book you can loose yourself, something which is being instilled into my grandchildren. Once you open up a book you are transported into a different world and can use your imagination. Sometimes laughing out loud and sometimes getting a tissue.

The trouble is your forget everything around you and time is just abandoned, something my mother would often do that's why she wasn't a very good cook. She was always burning things, leaving pans on the cooker to boil dry, with the acrid smell of burning wafting through the house. Today of course she would set off the smoke alarm but we didn't have them in those days.

When my mother used to visit us she would always offer to make a cup of tea. I told my daughter to watch her one day. She would put the kettle on, come back into the lounge, sit down pick up a crossword, or magazine and start to get carried away. The kettle would click off and that's as far as she got every time, she was so predictable. It was usually me who ended up making the tea and she would look so surprised when offering her a cup, "oh have you made the tea then dear" was her retort. Mother would often bring with her a cake or two, but bless her they were usually squashed in a paper bag and the icing or cream, would be stuck to the inside of the paper. She meant well and her offerings were appreciated and eaten.

Coffee on the other hand is always very nice on a trip out somewhere with a friend, or daughter. My eldest daughter Julie having a taste for black coffee is extremely fussy as to which coffee she drinks, so we have scouted around to find the best places in our local vicinity. As for me, tea is what I really prefer. My youngest daughter Caroline drinks only herbal teas, so herbal teas are kept in the house for when she visits.

Not being one for cream cakes or sticky buns, a scone or biscuit will usually suffice, but my eldest daughter just loves them without cream. The stickier the bun is the better she likes it, especially if it is a chocolate one. Now she has got her young daughter Rosie into girlie coffee trips, she doesn't drink coffee of course but she loves it when she is seated with at least two adults and is served with a drink and a sticky bun. She is the next shopaholic in the family, I can see it coming.

If we should go to buy shoes Rosie would sit on the floor with shoes all around her trying them on. Then she goes over to the clothes rails and says "that one is nice Mummy" in the hope that she will be in for a treat, she has her mother round her little finger! Does this remind me of anyone? Yes, my daughters and me with my mother, or grandmother.

We are at the garden centre where Deborah my eldest daughter's friend will be joining us for coffee. All the maps of Disney are placed on the table and we start our chat, being lost in an adventure we have yet to have in Disney. Deborah has already been there a few times and is telling us which are the best places to eat and to take children to, and the best rides, and all about the shows etc. I did ask her if she had over a month out there as there seems to be so much to do and so little time to do it all in. Two weeks, but very hectic she tells us.

We change the subject slightly and begin to talk about holidays Deborah and her family had with my daughter Julie and some of the things that have happened while they were away.

On one trip Julie and her husband Duncan took their caravan to Wells next the sea where they were due to meet up with Deborah and her family, who were already there in a static caravan. While they were on route they got a puncture in one of the caravan wheels. Duncan unhooked the caravan and took off in the car leaving Julie and the children in the caravan. It was pouring with rain at this time. He tried to find somewhere that would supply him with a replacement tyre, or at least be able to repair his tyre.

He eventually found a tyre fix company on an industrial estate which seemed deserted and in the middle of nowhere. There were no lights on but the door was open, so he walked inside only to set the alarm bells off. He was startled at the suddenness of the alarm but carried on looking around to see if he could find someone.

The next thing he saw was blue flashing lights coming closer. He wondered who they were after. The Police got out of their cars and vans and arrested him. Once he had explained that the building was open and there was no one about, they cautioned him and let him go on his way.

Julie at this time still didn't know what was happening and wondering where he had got to. Duncan finally rang her mobile and she couldn't believe what he told her. The Police spoke to her to verify what Duncan was up to. Someone apparently had reported seeing a man in a red jacket entering the building and the alarm going off.

Deborah's husband Paul came out from the caravan site to meet Duncan to see if he could help and they eventually got a wheel the right size and put it on, and finally continued on their journey. This was all before the holiday had started.

It all reminded me of a holiday we had once with my mother and my two daughters, where we stayed in a caravan at Bournemouth when they were young. It rained for days and the river where the site was located was beginning to flood. We sat and watched from the caravan window and saw some ducks spinning round in circles unable to swim down the river properly, as it was flowing so fast.

The girls and me in the caravan

That night my mother took a sleeping tablet and was almost out of it when we had a knock on the door, a man in a boat told us to evacuate and get up to the school building, as the banks were breached.

flood

I made some black coffee and took it to my mother who was very sleepy at the time. The girls tried to rouse her and encouraged her to drink the coffee. We finally got her awake enough to get her into a boat and we were all taken off the site. The following morning we heard that a caravan had been swept away. It was very frightening and we were glad to get home on that occasion.

Chapter 2

MINE OR YOURS

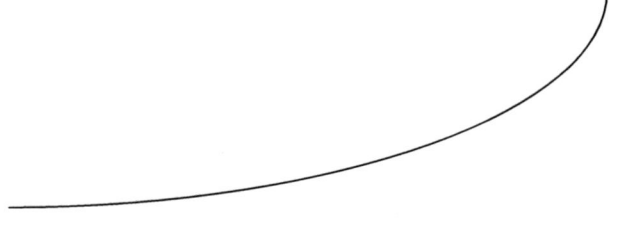

Have you ever worn odd shoes to work? Looking down at my feet whilst sitting at my desk I noticed one day that on one foot was a navy shoe and on the other a black shoe, at least they were the same style. Mike my husband, has worn slippers to work instead of shoes and had to come all the way back home again to change into shoes.

A navy and black shoe isn't so bad but when you wear odd trousers to a jacket – well. Mike once went to a function at his golf club. It was a dinner jacket do (DJ). When he came home he took off his jacket, then he realised that he had worn a casual blazer with his DJ trousers. Some time later after the social evening Mike said to his friend "why didn't you tell me I had an odd jacket on"? His friend said "I thought you knew". Having odd socks on is bad enough, especially when one is red and one is black, now that really is going too far not to notice.

Have you ever looked high and low for your glasses only to find that they are perched on top of your head? The times that has happened to me, having spent ages looking for them, they are on my head all the time.

It's the same with keys. Having turned all the drawers out looking for them, and turning my handbag inside out; there they are in my handbag after all. How come they don't fall out when you shake the bag upside down or turn the pockets inside out? Yet the next time you look they are nestling in there quite comfortably, sometimes even having the cheek to be lying on the bed, in full view. Someone's put them there, I know they have.

Some time ago there was a buzzer attached to

my keys so if I dialled a number it would ring, and I would know where they were. Unfortunately it has long gone now, but it was so useful. If my mobile goes missing I ring the number from a landline and of course when it rings it can be located, usually somewhere in the house.

In desperation sometimes when I really cannot find some item or other that has been mislaid, I ask my mother (who past away some years before) in silence; in my head – to help me find whatever it is; only to find it almost immediately. This almost freaks me out. How does she do it, is my mother still tuned into me?

We both worked in London's West End many years ago now when I was a single woman in my twenties, my mother would turn up to meet me for lunch and we would both have a gift for each other; something like a peach or some plums, and we would both have the same. We were very telepathic with each other; accept for when she would wear my clothes to work without me knowing.

Having come home from work early one day whilst still living at home, and hearing the key in the lock, she came through the door with my new coat on! When confronting her she just said I had good taste and that it was a compliment to me that she wanted to wear my clothes – well! Were they mine or hers? Talk about being caught out.

It transpired that she often used to wear my clothes. She should have known how I felt as she used to tell me about her sister wearing her clothes and stuffing them back into a drawer so she wouldn't find out, but of course she usually did.

I don't recall my daughters ever wearing my clothes, they would just wind me round their little fingers until I bought them what they wanted.

CHAPTER 3

A PASSION AT MY FEET

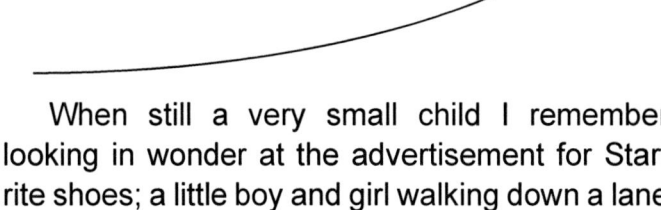

When still a very small child I remember looking in wonder at the advertisement for Start rite shoes; a little boy and girl walking down a lane hand in hand, with their new shoes and Dutch style hats on.

My first recollection of admiring footwear as a tiny tot was my brown T bar leather sandals, with crepe soles. Every summer I had a pair exactly the same as the previous year. Then one year quite out of the blue, my mother bought me a *red* pair, same style same T bar up the front of the foot, with little silver buckles to the side of the strap. The same stitching round the sole and same crepe soles. But what joy - *red* sandals.

Whenever I took them off they would be put side by side and just to look at them gave me a delighted sensation. I stood my white socks up inside each of the sandals so it looked as though I had just stepped out of them. This was the beginning of a shoe fetish.

Around the age of about eleven years old and having saved enough money - I went shopping to buy a pair of black, backless slippers with velvet across the front, and gold and coloured embroidery across them. Oh they were so beautiful. Having bought them from Woolworths in Kingsbury for eleven shillings and nine pence (about 56 pence today) my money was well spent. They were so cheap but to me they were the most luxurious slippers ever. They were filled with what sounded and felt like reed and had soft leather soles. I bought several pairs as they didn't last long.

When we were very young teenagers my Nan took my cousin Gillian and me to Westcliffe on Sea for a holiday, we were staying with Nan's friends' daughter Mary who ran the guest house, and while we were there she took us to Pittsea

Market. We had taken the train as it was a long way from where we were staying.

Once we were at the market and having made a bee line for the sandals, I spotted a pair of canvas red and white stripped ones, with a small wedge heel and a sling back strap. Would Nan buy them for me I wondered? Yes she did. Then spotting a navy and white pair the same style, there was no way we could leave without this pair also. "No" Nan said "one pair is enough" but not being able to leave it there, and my pleading not going unnoticed; both pairs ended up in my arms in brown paper bags, a big smile spreading across my face. Nothing could give me as much pleasure as those lovely sandals; which I wore constantly. I must have walked round with my head downwards most of that summer.

I felt very guilty at twisting my Nan round my little finger and making her buy me both pairs, but promised that she would be paid back every penny out of my pocket money when it had been earned.

Having saved all my pocket money whilst still at school; the first pair of shoes I bought myself were black suede moccasins, slip on shoes – what joy, no more lace ups for me. With white socks they looked o.k. but felt marvellously grown up. At twelve going on thirteen at the time I wore them to school.

Then it was high heels - at only fourteen. Mother took me to Kingsbury to buy my first pair of grown up shoes with heels. Being overjoyed, it soon turned sour when she insisted on buying me a pair of Cuban heeled shoes, beige ones, with little heels that were actually very difficult to balance in. No, five inch stiletto heeled shoes in cream; the ones that were displayed in the window were the ones for me. We argued in the shop. Mother purchased those awful Cuban heeled shoes which I wouldn't wear. And never did wear them.

Doing a Saturday morning job enabled me to save enough money to buy the cream stiletto heeled shoes for thirty nine shillings and eleven pence old money (approximately £1.50 pence today) and wore them home. I remember wearing them to school on my last day; with a dress Nan had made me which had a boat neckline and a full skirt, with a cummerbund round the waist. It was white with turquoise roses all over it and my net petticoat underneath to hold the skirt out.

This reminded me of my first paper nylon petticoat which was bought for me as a birthday gift from my Aunty Jean. The excitement at this wonderful gift was overwhelming. It was so pretty with pale blue embroidery on the top layer and it rustled so loudly when I walked. I ran upstairs with it on and ran down to hear it rustle, and see it billow in the breeze. Having done this over and over again my mother and Aunty Jean told me to stop running up and down the stairs and put some clothes on.

I wore it to school one day underneath my school dress. My teacher called me out to the front of the class. He then sent me to the back of the class and told everyone to be quiet. All that could be heard was the rustling of my petticoat. Giggling broke out as he asked me to take the register, and then walk back to my seat.

Another time; having purchased yards of coloured net, and making myself a blue net petticoat, in several gathered layers. My friend Pat loved it, and asked me to make her one in yellow, which I did. It was the fashion at that time after paper nylon petticoats; it was net layered petticoats to hold a skirt out.

The seeds had been well and truly sewn for me becoming a shopaholic. It gave me such immense pleasure to trawl round the fabric shop in Kingsbury and browse through the umpteen rolls of material, thinking of what I could make. Just to feel all the fabrics was a delight. (I must have a vivid imagination).

Shoes however, have been a passion of mine all my life. At one time there were more than 100 pairs of slippers, shoes, sandals and boots in the cupboard. In the loft still wrapped in tissue paper, are my black satin stiletto heeled, pointed toed shoes that I wore for dancing as a teenager, along with my old ice skates. I just can't bring myself to throw them away, although my feet don't fit in them any more and I couldn't walk in them anyway now. But every now and again they are loving put on my feet for me to look at and try and imagine how on earth I ever walked in them.

The trouble is its like tops; having bought them and put them away in the cupboard they get forgotten. Then the following year I buy new ones to go with such and such outfit. Only to find when it is time to get out all the summer things, there they are all brand new, still with their price tags attached, which means that I can now go shopping to make up a whole outfit; with shoes and bag perhaps. What a good idea.

I still cannot come to terms with the fact that good shoes would cost 49/11d back in the fifties, but today would cost £40 there is no justification in this at all. Money just doesn't seem to go anywhere these days. You just need so much of it, and the pound coins weigh so heavy in your purse.

CHAPTER 4

GLITTERY THINGS

My ears were pierced at the age of fifteen. Having taken the bus one lunch hour from Edgware where I was working, to another part of town, I went into a jewellers shop that advertised ear piercing. Having paid my money and sat down, a towel was put round my neck and my ears were duly pierced with a needle. Gold sleepers were put in straight away. To me they looked beautiful. I had wanted pierced ears for years. My Nan had said she had always wanted pierced ears but had never got round to it, so she wore screw on earrings, or clip on earrings.

When it was time to go home after a days work, the weather had turned very cold. It was November so I should have expected it. My ears began to hurt while standing at the bus stop, so I turned my coat collar up. My hair was tied back in a pony tail and my ears were exposed to the cold air. By the time I got home they were burning so badly and were all bright red and swollen.

Pouring some antiseptic liquid into a bowl with hot water and mixing the two together I bathed my ears with cotton wool. The relief was wonderful, although sleep wouldn't come that night. Every time I went to lie on my side, my ears would hurt and wake me up. So the bathing went on for days and slowly I began to turn the sleepers round and my ears began to heal.

The clip on earrings I had bought previously would no longer be worn. There were so many pairs of clip on earrings which had been bought from a local Woolworths store for about a shilling in old money (5 pence today) I couldn't bear to part with some of them, as one or two pairs were bought for me from friends. So they were left in the bottom of a little glass pot. Shopping for a collection of new earrings had begun.

On one occasion my granddad wanted to take his little poodle dog called Mitzie to the poodle parlour to have her clipped. We went together on the bus. He put on his smart grey gabardine raincoat and did the belt up, (something as children we never did - I can hear my mother saying "do your belt up"). I put something special on and tied my hair up in a pony tail, as we were going into Reading. It was drummed into us that we should always look smart when we went out especially with Nan or Granddad. Mitzie was duly clipped to her red leather lead and off we set. We waited ages for the bus and took the long ride into town.

Having walked round Reading until we came to the poodle parlour, we deposited Mitzie the little dog who looked terrified. We told the lady we would pick her up in about an hour or so.

Off we went to the shops. We had a coffee first then walked round looking into the shop windows. Standing outside a jewellers shop looking at earrings, granddad asked me what I was looking at, so having shown him the little ruby earrings set in a circle of gold, with butterfly backs. He did no more than open the shop door and the bell tinkled as he walked in, with me behind him.

He asked the shopkeeper to fetch the little earrings he had seen me looking at in the window. Turning them over in my hand granddad said he would buy them for me and asked the man to put them in a box. I couldn't believe it – I must have been very spoilt. He paid the seven shillings and six pence old money(35pence today) and there were the beautiful gold earrings with a ruby stone, in a small packet in my hands. They are over fifty years old now and are still treasured. When I look at them it reminds me of that day with my granddad.

My dearest grandparents

It was a different story when both my daughters Julie and Caroline wanted their ears pierced. My youngest daughter Caroline went into the jewellers at the top of our road and I went with her. The lady was very nervous and after she had done one ear, she had a problem doing the other. Caroline went very white and almost passed out. One ear was pierced higher than the other and my daughter was devastated. She didn't keep her sleepers in and her ears closed up, and she doesn't wear earrings now.

My other daughter Julie had her ears done with no problem, why is it that some people have rotten bad luck whilst others sail through life?

My jewellery box is overflowing with earrings but you can guarantee that if a pair is expensive you will lose one, and if you have a cheap pair they will last and last. It's always, always the most expensive earrings that you lose.

The first pair of plain gold earrings I possessed were little gold birds, beautiful little Swallows with wings outstretched. I wore them when on holiday with my friend Margaret. We were both seventeen years old at the time and staying in Austria. One fell down the plug hole in the sink in our room as I tried to put it in.

Trying to explain what had happened to the maids proved very difficult, but we must have managed it, as some time later the maid knocked on the door with my little earring in her hand. It was absolutely wonderful to be reunited with it.

The pair are still in my jewellery box today and that was well over forty five years ago.

When I look at them it reminds me of the holiday with my friend Margaret being half way up a mountain in Austria with tiny snowballs in our hands. We were both very impressed with our first holiday abroad. We had our first cable car ride and felt very grown up to be abroad on our own.

Chapter 5

VACUUM SEALED

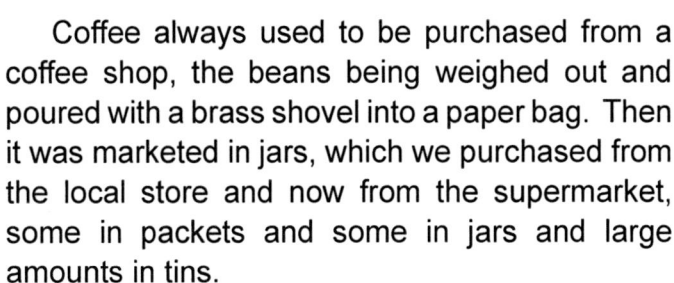

Coffee always used to be purchased from a coffee shop, the beans being weighed out and poured with a brass shovel into a paper bag. Then it was marketed in jars, which we purchased from the local store and now from the supermarket, some in packets and some in jars and large amounts in tins.

Packaging was beginning to change but my

mother hadn't realised this. She bought a packet of ground coffee in a red and gold packet, which had been air sealed. When she got home she took the packet out of her basket and went to put it into the cupboard but it felt hard, so she went all the way back to the shops and complained to the Manager that the coffee was 'off'. No he explained - "yes" she said - it was solid – "feel the packet". He opened the bag to show my mother that the coffee was in fact vacuum sealed to keep it fresh. She felt such a fool and was so embarrassed; but she said he was such a nice man.

Things are definitely getting more and more difficult to open, like those silly little pots of milk that go everywhere when you do finally get the top off them, and now they have brought out those tubes of milk that definitely go everywhere, accept in the cup. Or is it me. I always had to open the milk pots for my mother, so now it's my daughter's turn to open them for me. Even my grandson has trouble opening up a sachet of tomato sauce with more on the table than on the plate.

SHRINKAGE

Having bought a white angora sweater once, that was so soft and fluffy and felt gorgeous next to my skin, I washed it and it wouldn't have fitted a baby, let alone me when it was dry. What a waste of money. I shan't be buying another angora sweater.

It reminded me of when, having spent hours knitting a sweater when about thirteen years old. I finally finished it and having sewn it up and put the buttons on I wore it – with pride. Then washed it, the same thing happened; having shrunk it wouldn't have fitted a child. It came out like a piece of cardboard and ended up in the dustbin. It had taken me weeks to knit too. Yet another time when my eldest daughter Julie was about one year old I knitted her a dress which, when washed, would stretch – she was still wearing it when she was two years old!

Chapter 6

TEACAKE ANYONE?

Its time for a teacake, you go and order. I got a taste for toasted teacakes while on the first holiday with Mike my husband, at Lytham St Anne's, near Blackpool. We had gone to a little café which had 'Olde Worlde' windows, little square ones with rows and rows of teapots in the window, on the shelf inside.

We went in and sat down and ordered toasted teacakes. They were delicious and I was hooked.

Now its toasted teacakes with a coffee whenever we go out. Scones are alright but a teacake is not quite so dry on the pallet.

Haven't things changed – a coffee used to be just that; coffee with milk in a jug so that you could pour in the amount you wanted. Now its cappuccino, latte, espresso, Americana, mocha, mocha latte, white with milk, black; small, regular, and large, I am in awe of the choices today. We have so much choice it just causes confusion, well I get confused easily anyway. Tea what would you like? Earl grey, Green tea, Darjeeling, breakfast tea, English tea - oh my goodness here we go again. I just want a cup of tea. Do you want it with milk, without milk, with sugar without sugar, with sweetener or with out, or do you want honey? The choice is endless and I am getting thirsty.

Then its eggs, eggs over easy! Sunny side up, fried, poached, steamed, boiled, coddled or scrambled. It just proves how eggs are so versatile; no I'll have an omelette instead!

How I remember just after the war – we had virtually no food whatsoever in our larder at home. Food was still being rationed and I remember the ration books well. My mother would walk at least two miles to the shops and queue for hours outside the bakers for a six penny bun round, which was always our treat on a Saturday.

Sometimes my brother and I would be sent up the road for one, it was like a lot of white iced buns stuck together in a circle, it was the cheapest cake we could afford at that time, and as mother wasn't very good at making cakes we preferred the 'iced bun round'. Home made cakes were a rarity in those days. Something we only had at my grandmothers.

We didn't have a fridge in those early days, just a meat safe which stood on the concrete floor of the larder. It was just a box with a wire door with a knob for a handle. It was when my mother took a piece of beef out of it one day, and a blue bottle fly flew past her that she looked closer at it, and there were the eggs, so it had to be thrown away. My father bought us a fridge that week.

We had so little yet we were satisfied, as we weren't aware of the choices other people had. Not so much in this country at that time but certainly in America. We were about to become more like Americans with greater choices.

We still grew most of our produce in the gardens and a lot of people had allotments which I notice are now back in fashion, with everyone going 'green'. The vegetables we grew successfully were runner beans, courgettes and marrows. Then deciding to grow a pineapple, it grew and it got so large and the leaves were so sharp; my eldest daughter's dog was always knocking it over, it eventually ended up in the bin.

Which reminds me of my daughters when they were small and would start to grow cress on the window sill, then it was onions and carrot tops. We grew potatoes once and they were not successful as we had blight in them and had to throw them all away. Thinking about it I will stick to the farm shop or the local supermarket. We do have a fig tree in the garden that was bird seed dropping, but it does produce figs every year.

Another occasion my daughter Julie who was two at the time, and dressed in her little pink fluffy coat, with a hood; was running about up the garden waving her arms about shouting out "buddy fies, buddy fies". Oh! I really must be more careful what I say within ear shot of her. Having been up the garden earlier in the day and noticing the flies on my sprouts; I must have waved my arms about and shouted "bloody flies", which of course she had copied. So how could I be cross with her, I had to explain that she shouldn't say it, but you can see how the confusion in small children can take effect, it's so difficult to curb your words and make sure they are not in earshot.

Mother and Julie in her pink fluffy coat

You can guarantee that the words they shouldn't repeat are the ones they do repeat and the ones they should, they don't.

Don't they just remind you when they are older – "no" you say "I never said that" "Oh yes you did" "you always used to say it". Did I really, well I don't remember (I'm getting older and am forgetful – that's my excuse).

Chapter 7

IF I CAN REMEMBER

Moving on to more recent times I went through a phase of vomiting - every time Mike and I went out. Our friend Nick said to my husband "every time, every time you go out she's sick" and so I was.

Once we went to a wedding and I was sick in

the evening after eating a meal. Everything was going round and round and I felt dreadful. It was a good thing we had a room booked at the hotel the wedding was held in. Mike wouldn't leave me and therefore he missed all the dancing and celebrating.

The following morning feeling like nothing on earth and still retching as by this time there was nothing left in my stomach (Mike thought I had done it on purpose; of course I hadn't-silly man). He didn't speak to me much that day which was just as well as I didn't feel like chatting for a change.

We had been out with Nick and Jane on one occasion and when we got back to their house Nick poured me a drink. Unbeknown to me he had mixed the drink deliberately to see what reaction he would get from me!! And it was potent. Having had the drink it wasn't too long before I was feeling terrible and being sick all through the night and the following morning.

After staying the night at their house, Mike was up bright and early the next morning ready to go home. On coming downstairs I pulled a chair out and sat at the kitchen table and hung my head. Nick laughed at me and said "I have never seen anyone actually green before" I looked and felt dreadful.

On the way home Mike had to stop the car for me to be sick on the verge. It transpired that Nick had mixed the drink for fun – well I won't be letting him get me a drink again in a hurry.

Once we were invited to a Christmas meal celebration in a hotel with the people Mike worked for at the time. Having been very sick before we left and not really feeling like going out, I had to pull myself together for Mike's sake, so got myself bathed and changed.

Mike had cleaned the car and got it looking pristine inside and out, so in we got and off we set, only for me to say "pull in I'm going to be sick" he didn't pull in quick enough. So with my head out the window while he was still driving, it splashed all over the side of his nice clean, shiny car. He didn't say a word so I knew he was devastated.

We arrived at the hotel and went into the lounge area with me looking as white as a sheet; everyone was commenting on how pale I looked. We stayed for a short while then we made our apologies and left just after the meal, which hadn't been eaten. Mike took me home and I went to bed.

On another occasion my daughter Julie and I went away for a weekend to the Cotswold as she needed a break. Not knowing at the time that I was allergic to pork! We had a meal of roast pork and I was so sick and ill all through the night and was still being ill the following morning at gone 10am. A doctor was called at about 11am. The hotel wanted to clean the room for the next guests and kept ringing our room to see if we were ready to leave.

My daughter Julie and the porter had a struggle to get me into the car; then she had to drive all the way home. What a weekend that was.

It did seem that for a while I really was always sick when we went out. Was I becoming unsociable, or was it something subconscious. Or was it that not being a drinker, alcohol really doesn't agree with me, and even a glass of wine shouldn't pass my lips. It seemed to be a phase I went through.

My eldest grandson Ben is taking after me, he is always ill if we are going anywhere special, particularly at the airport. He is usually the one laid out on the seats, with his head in his hands. With him it's possibly nerves, with me maybe my age has something to do with it.

Have you ever had a bruise that you don't remember getting? Most people have I suppose. A huge bruise appeared on my shoulder once, along with a broken finger nail and a bent and very painful finger on the other hand. Having collapsed in the bathroom and blacked out completely, I woke up to find myself on the floor but didn't know my shoulder had hit anything until the following day when I saw this black bruise on my skin.

Some people get bruises on their legs without knowing how they got there. Mike's mother was always getting bruises and very nasty ones too, they put it down to her having diabetes.

I hope I am not going to start blacking out as my mother did. She fell over in the street once and badly hurt her eye, but on that occasion it was the pavements being so uneven. Does the brain give up slowly? Or is it lack of concentration. I really should like to know.

When at twenty two I kept passing out, an ECG was arranged and the hospital told me it was the stress of my forthcoming wedding and being underweight and that nothing else was wrong. Well it certainly isn't being underweight nowadays!

Chapter 8

NIGHT SCHOOL

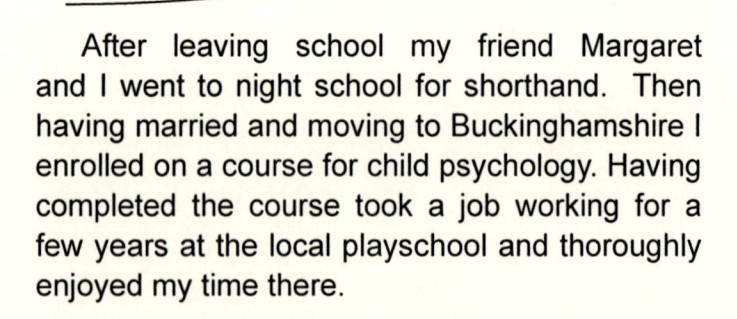

After leaving school my friend Margaret and I went to night school for shorthand. Then having married and moving to Buckinghamshire I enrolled on a course for child psychology. Having completed the course took a job working for a few years at the local playschool and thoroughly enjoyed my time there.

The next course I enrolled for was an art course. We had a male model who was an old man with a beard. Having sketched him first on a large washed piece of paper, I then painted him. It took weeks to complete and being very proud of my painting, bought a frame for it, but haven't a clue where it is today.

I also did some line drawing when the painting was finished and really got a flare for it. I ended up sketching at home and did a picture of my second husband asleep on the chair. It was quite good even if I say so myself.

Having tried calligraphy another time, I didn't get on too well with it although the pens are still in the cupboard, should I decide to try again. Pottery was another course; actually there were two courses, one with my daughter Julie and one on my own. They were enjoyable and my pots and bits and pieces were much treasured.

Then I signed up for Italian language lessons and was getting on quite well with it, until the teacher went to the end of the book we were following, and totally confused some of us. So I didn't enrol for the next session and gave that up. It was a shame as one of the girls in the class would 'phone me each week, or I would phone her and we would speak in Italian to each other for practise. I have lost it all now which is a pity, it's such a pretty language.

The next course was reflexology and a ten week course on aromatherapy and massage, which was really enjoyable. The books and the oils are still in my silver case. I went with a friend but she got funny with me at our exercise classes once because she didn't like me turning up (in the summer) in shorts, as did several other women, due to the heat. She almost shouted at me - how dare I turn up in shorts showing all my legs. She got so nasty I stopped seeing her. At least I finished the courses.

Which reminds me of an earlier time when my girls were very small, and we had a party for women. My friend at the time pressed her self against me in a manner I didn't feel comfortable with. She asked to borrow a summer flared patterned trouser suit to wear to a party she was going to, when she asked me for it again I got a niggling feeling and so ended our friendship. She moved away soon afterwards thank goodness.

On another subject entirely - When I was very young my father was balding so he believed that cranial massage was the answer to his problems. He bought no end of bottles with different coloured liquid in them, some oils and some lotions. He had a whole box of them.

He made me stand at the back of his armchair and I had to pour a little of the oil in my hand

and massage this into his scalp. It was almost a nightly ritual; there I would stand massaging away until I decided to give him tiny plaits all over his head one day. This was great fun especially when someone knocked at the door and asked for him and he couldn't get the plaits out quickly enough. Can you imagine how he must have felt going to the door with plaits in his hair? He looked ridiculous but unfortunately for me it didn't stop him making me massage his head again.

Then one day wanting to go out to play and because he wouldn't let me, I dug my nails into his scalp. At which point he yelled at me and I was let off the massaging that night, thank goodness. I said "Oh I'm so sorry Dad" liar - I hated doing it every night and couldn't stand the smell of the oils, but I had a guilt feeling for some time afterwards at what I had done.

Chapter 9

TOO MUCH OR NOT ENOUGH

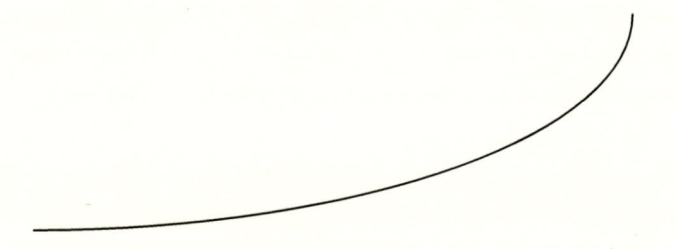

Having just been informed by my youngest grandson Theo that I am only a Grandma and I'm not very old, it's made me feel good. "You are not a Granny yet" he told me, "Grannies are old, you're not old, you are only a Grandma." "You are not old up to the world"! Whatever that means, bless him, so I'm not old, thank goodness for that, and don't have white curly hair either, he told me (which I don't). So now I can do my keep fit knowing that I am not doing it to keep *supple* but for the sake of *toning* my body. Not to keep arthritis at bay but for the good of my health to keep me young.

Well we do live and learn from our grandchildren. Looking after young Theo one afternoon, he went into my bedroom to see my suitcase on the bed ready for my pending holiday. "Wow Grandma, how are you going to get all that into your suitcase"?" "I'm not" I said, "The clothes in that pile are going to be worn on the journey, and these in this pile are going into the case". "Oh that's such a lot of clothes" he said.

Well having told my husband that I didn't need anything new for the pending holiday and only taking enough for one week, as we could wash things out and wear them for the next week.

Meeting my friend Anne at the shops was my downfall, and of course saw just what I wanted. A pair of cropped trousers, a jumper and two nighties' – to replace the ones that I had ironed a hole in earlier in the year. So there were a few more items to put in the case than had been intended. But it was Anne's fault for making me walk round the shops! Isn't it nice to blame someone else for your shopping addiction?

We were doing our coffee and chat routine at

the shops. Anne bought a duvet, duvet cover, skirt and umpteen other things; so we were loaded up with bags when we went into the store for coffee. It took an age to get the bags to stay upright. The duvet had a mind of its own and kept rolling over. We eventually stuffed it in between the glass panelled wall and the table.

We had missed our shopping sprees as we had been meeting for lunch at an eatery which kept us from shopping, so it was glorious to spend with the excuse that I was going on holiday. So I needed some new things to wear, but what was Anne's excuse?

How many times have you gone into a shop to buy a specific item, got inside and forgotten what you went in for, and come out with arm loads of bags and umpteen things you didn't want in the first place. I'm always doing it. It seems to be a woman thing, or is it?

My husband Mike will come shopping with me on the odd occasion and always put things in the basket we don't need. If we go into a sports shop he will always find some golf thing or other that he just has to have. So perhaps it's not just a woman thing after all, they just tell you it is in the hope that the next time you go shopping you will think twice about purchasing items.

My mother had the right idea she would say "if it's exactly what you want, don't look at the price, but if it's not exactly what you want, study the price". What do you earn money for anyway if you can't indulge yourself now and again? Life shouldn't be all about bills and more bills, the unforeseen bills like car maintenance and repairs in the home, plus the regular bills that is so boring.

It always seems that you no sooner have a little nest egg than something needs replacing or repairing.

New taps have to be put in the kitchen, and on the bath and bathroom sink. I don't have the strength in my hands to turn the taps on and off that are in situ at the moment. So new ones have been purchased and I am waiting for the plumber to arrive to do the work.

That's a minor setback; it's the car that costs the most. So I don't feel bad about having a 'spend up' now and again, what's the point of saving, it will be paid out again on bills anyway. In one hand and out the other - that's life! Shall we have another coffee with a bun this time?

Chapter 10

ONE IN THE EYE

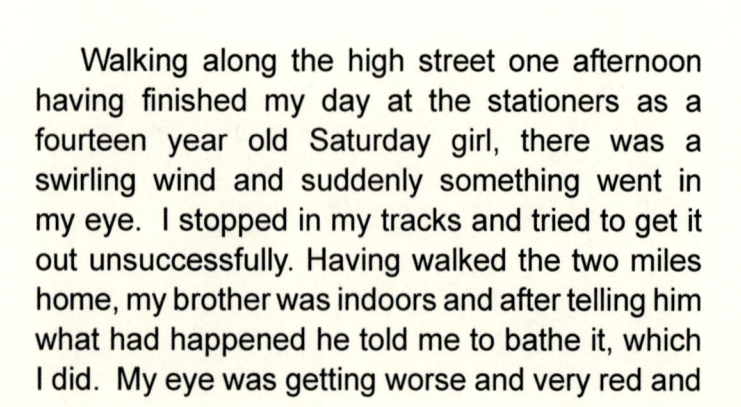

Walking along the high street one afternoon having finished my day at the stationers as a fourteen year old Saturday girl, there was a swirling wind and suddenly something went in my eye. I stopped in my tracks and tried to get it out unsuccessfully. Having walked the two miles home, my brother was indoors and after telling him what had happened he told me to bathe it, which I did. My eye was getting worse and very red and sore. Mother came home and said it would be alright if I bathed it.

Having mentioned to my brother later that day that I couldn't see properly, he looked at my eye and said he was taking me to the hospital. He asked my mother for the loan of her Lambretta. "You don't need to go to the hospital" she said "if there is anything in there it will come out by itself, it can't be much as she can still open and close her eye". My brother told me to get on the back of the scooter and off we went to the local hospital.

It turned out after having blue dye put in my eye that there was in fact a tiny piece of metal lodged in the eyeball. No wonder it hurt so much. I came out of hospital with a pad over my eye and some cream to put on it the following day. When we got home my mother said it wasn't necessary to have gone to the hospital, it would have come out by itself.

I have never understood her, she was the nicest person you could meet but whenever there was something wrong with me, she was very hard and very seldom sympathetic. As a child it would be my father who would carry me to the bathroom if I had been ill in bed, or carry me into the house if I had fallen over and cut myself outside, never my mother. It seemed as though she closed up when someone had an accident, and yet she was a Red

Cross nurse during the war.

Out in the garden recently something flew into my eye and bathing it didn't get it out, trying not to rub it – memories of childhood. As my eye was getting so painful my husband drove me to the local hospital; there was a thorn stuck in the inside of my eyelid, which wouldn't come out with bathing and was scratching the eye every time I blinked. My eye was quite swollen and very red. It was pulled out by a lovely Caribbean doctor, who made me laugh. (Actually he made me go weak at knees but don't tell anyone). He made me do all sorts of eye movements and said it would take about a week to heal as the eye ball was badly scratched; there were two pieces stuck in the eye but he got them out.

Anyway having come out of the hospital with a patch on, this time my husband didn't seem too bothered. We went into an Indian restaurant for a meal and bumped into the doorway as I couldn't see where I was going as the good eye was swollen too. But the doorman was wonderful and so helpful; and after me tripping on a small ledge under the doorway, I finally went through a revolving door into the restaurant.

It seemed I was an embarrassment as when the waiter came to the table, the silly man stood at the side of me with the eye patch on, and of course couldn't see him, so couldn't order. Did no one understand! My husband is and my mother was - *Piscean*- making decisions then changing their minds, sympathetic and distant all in one go, very confusing.

Thinking about it my brother looked after me quite well. Once I was invited to a party, an engagement party for the girl at work, when I was fifteen and didn't get home until 3am in the morning. It was only a small party with mainly her family and just a few friends. Unbeknown to me my brother had cycled to where he thought the party was being held to pick me up and bring me home. But I wasn't at the address he went to.

Apparently there had been a broken window at another house where Police were called. Not finding me there, he cycled home and he and my mother were beside themselves. When my brother; again on his bicycle, came riding up the road later in the night he saw me calmly walking home arm in arm with a boy from the engagement party we had been to. He was being kind enough to escort me all the way home. I got a telling off from both my brother and my mother once inside.

Having explained where the party was and having shown my brother the invitation with the address on it, he realised I wasn't at the rowdy party in another road. I was never in as late as that again. So they did worry about me which was nice in a way. It wasn't restrictive as I didn't go out late to parties much, until I was a bit older anyway.

Me at 21

At my twenty first we were doing the Conga down the road at 2am. Parties in those days were wonderful, dancing all night long. People didn't get as drunk as they seem to now and everyone had a great time. Music was great to dance to and sing along to, we were all friends and it was a good crowd to be with. There aren't many songs I can sing along to today, but can remember almost all the words of songs from the sixties and seventies.

My grandchildren are surprised when I start to sing to the tunes they are beginning to play on their guitars. The tunes are slightly different but the words are usually much the same. Yes, even an ancient like me can sing along to a familiar tune.

The oldest song I remember is one my mother would sing to me as a tiny child, it was an Irish Lullaby - Toora loora something Hush now don't you cry. I don't remember many of the words but can remember the tune and see her stroking my hair and singing in a soft voice.

Having decided to hold a party, the arrangements were made and the party duly held. I wanted my friend Jo to meet the boy who worked in my office as she had a bad experience of someone letting her down. He didn't even have the guts to face her but left her note in her room. So she needed cheering up and the party was arranged with the intention they should both meet.

They did and got on very well. They had plenty of time to get to know each other as the party went on for some time and the last train had gone, so they all stayed the night and we sat up talking until some people fell asleep in their chairs.

A relationship blossomed and they eventually married; we attended the service and reception. They went on to have two little boys. Unfortunately for me we lost touch soon afterwards.

Jo was my bridesmaid at my wedding. I met her through our mothers; they had been friends years earlier and lost touch. Then Jo's family moved to our road in Kingsbury, and when my mother met up with her mother they were delighted; and so they resumed their friendship and Jo and I became good friends.

We both worked in the West End of London at one time, Jo in Baker Street and me just off Oxford Street. We would meet up every week for lunch and go into a bistro somewhere.

We stayed with each other on a Wednesday night. Jo's mum always brought breakfast up to me in my room the following morning, which was such a treat for me as my mother by then was living in America. Jo wasn't so lucky when she stayed with me; her breakfast was in the kitchen with me the following morning, then on the train and off to work.

We both excelled at dressmaking which was a hobby of mine and Jo's. In those days we made everything we wore and were up to the minute in fashion. Working in London we had access to the best shops and enjoyed life to the full.

Me and Jo

Chapter 11

HAVE I BEEN THERE ALREADY?

We're back from Disney and have been back several days already and I still can't get back into the rhythm of sleep. Having been to the dentist today I've had a sneaky cat nap to try and catch up. Since being home again I'm talking all funny, or at least it feels as though I am and can't slow down.

Mike and I took my daughters, their husbands

and all the grandchildren to Orlando, Florida for a two week holiday to Disney – all twelve of us. We left from Gatwick and arrived at our luxury five star hotel. Our rooms were next to each other along the corridor, so the balconies were all in a row, so we could lean over them and talk to each other. We had picnics on the balcony sometimes and other times we all merged on one balcony for drinks; whilst the children watched TV.

No one seemed very well on arrival and we found ourselves at the Drop in Clinic in town. Julies youngest Rosie had been the day before and was whisked off late at night with Julie by ambulance to a children's hospital the other side of Orlando. Julie didn't have a phone with her and no one knew where she had gone.

Poor little Rosie was on a drip all night and the following day. The others were all given medication but Rosie wasn't well at all. Having found out where they were. Mike, Duncan, little Theo and me spent all day at the hospital, while Caroline and Richard took Ben and Josh to the pictures with their children Brandon and Liam. But like all children Rosie bounced back in a few days and it was all forgotten.

We had a few mishaps such as loosing the paperwork for the cars, loosing the zipper folder which housed all the passports, money and cards etc. The room keys not working for us to get through the barrier with the cars. We went to the Retail Centre and someone had a strop and walked out of the store – no it wasn't me. I had managed to buy a bag and some earrings.

The first thing we wanted to do was visit The Magic Kingdom. We took the boat across the lake from the car park and as the castle came into view it was thrilling and exciting. We had all ages with us from eleven years down to three years so we had the perfect excuse for not going on the big rides. We took the train ride and visited this theme park twice.

Mike and me outside the Magic Kingdom

We have seen the most wonderful shows and had magical journeys. The parades were just wonderful and certainly captivated the children. The little ones enjoyed a ride on a pink sea shell which ran along a railway line and we had Nemo and Doris swimming about in 3D in front of us as we went on our journey at Epcot; and the boys had a go on a space ride.

Everyone had clubbed together to buy Mike a round of golf for his birthday. Very nice and he enjoyed it and decided to go again.

On that day we all went to Blizzard beach and just enjoyed the relaxing atmosphere. There were cable cars and I said I would like to go on one but how do you get down? Richard informed me there was a gentle ride down in a rubber ring!! Gentle my foot.

We took the cable car to the top and there were two choices of getting back down to ground level - one in the doughnut in which about six people sat, or you went by yourself on a massive water slide back down to the bottom. We chose the doughnut, we thought it was going to be like the lazy river ride (where you sit in a single rubber ring and gently float along the river) – no such luck, we went sideways and almost over the top of the ride path, then back down again and Julie and I were screaming and also got soaked. We seemed to get very wet most of the holiday.

Ben was taking some photographs and dropped his camera in the water. Duncan got hold of Josh and held him upside down over the railings until his arm went into the water up to his shoulder and he managed to retrieve the camera; but I shouldn't think it will be much good now. Josh was clapped by the crowd that had gathered. I think people must have wondered if Duncan was trying to drown his young son.

We went for a ride on a raft type boat at Sea World. I so wanted to go on a big ride and little Theo was looking after me; so he said he would come on the ride too. He was only just big enough to pass the height restriction limit. Mike didn't want to come. "If Theo can come then so can you" I told him. We stood in the queue and waited.

We began to think that maybe we had got into the wrong queue as there was a roller coaster ride next to us; and for a short while I wanted to turn and run. I was not going on that! We went through the gates at last and stood where we were meant to get on the raft for our Atlantis ride.

Was this meant to be enjoyable? Our Atlantis ride

Up we went round and up again. In the dark it was all very pretty with coloured lights in the ceiling. But I was not prepared for what was to come next. It was a sheer drop down to the bottom and we all screamed. My hair stood on end and thankfully I had the hats tucked into my top, otherwise I would have been soaked through. Mike and Duncan were sitting at the front with the boys behind them. They all got saturated. I was so proud of Theo but he was terrified of any other rides that holiday, so we had to keep finding little rides to build his confidence back up again.

We went to the animal Kingdom after it had been raining heavily and actually it was the best time to go. It felt like we were in a rainforest. We had a journey through the Wildlife Park on Safari. We took a train ride and had the most wonderful day but lost Josh at one point and that was worrying. We went to see the Nemo show here and it was well worth the wait, as it poured with rain whilst we were inside.

When they all went off the Kennedy Space Centre two of us went back to Blizzard Beach with the youngest children - unfortunately Mike cut his big toe rather badly and couldn't get about, so he had a quiet day at the hotel with his foot up. No more golf for that holiday. Not to be left out Rosie cut her toe and then Ben did the same!

Julie was the one that had most rides as hers included an ambulance ride through the night. We went on buses, safaris, monorail, steamboat, water raft rides, train rides, carousel rides, doughnut ring rides and cable car rides. Everything you can imagine. It was a great experience. There were so many wonderful shows we lost count of what we had seen and how many we went to.

Although it was a wonderful holiday, I would not want to travel for eight hours on a plane again with young children. The parents got too fraught, and grandma got too worried when children went out of sight.

The food wasn't my favourite but I did have my American burger at the poolside which was gorgeous, and I am not a burger type of person but must say it was enjoyable. That reminds me its time for something to eat. Oh I have been to the dentist and my mouth is still a little sore so will have some soup. It's so quiet here on my own I know I'm back. No little ones running in and out of our room and no big ones interrupting our romantic moments, by knocking on the door at an inappropriate time.

It's alright for Mike he is now thinking about his week's golf coming up very soon in Portugal, with his mates. How I could do with a weeks peaceful rest in Portugal. Hope his big toe is o.k. for all his golf; actually it amazes me that on the Saturday we got back he was able to play golf. He said he hobbled around the course – but he managed it! amazing.

Having mowed the lawns the day after we returned I mustn't complain. The garden is looking lovely now with all the daffodils out and the tulips are coming out too. My stone statue of a lady has been put out in the centre of the garden and it looks gorgeous and is encouraging me to go out there and do some weeding.

Duncan was very kind and came and changed my tap in the bathroom, so no more dripping taps. The plumber only did the kitchen tap. Duncan amazes me. Whenever he has a problem he gets on with it and sorts a problem out. He can turn his hand to anything plumbing, electrics, gardening and building.

When we picked the cars up at Gatwick on our return, he opened the window only to find it slid down and he couldn't get it back up again. He did no more than take the panel off the inside of the door and fixed it. He is brilliant to have around. Nothing seems to phase him; he will try and replace or repair anything.

Chapter 12

A CHANGE IN SHAPE

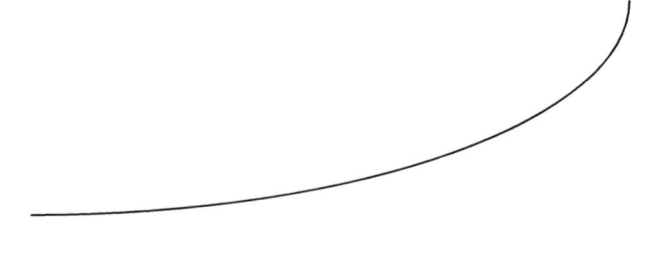

Have you noticed how people's shapes have changed over the years? The hour glass figure is well and truly gone. Most youngsters seem to have a curved back with a tummy. Is it the way they stand? Seeing an email that was doing the rounds some time ago, it showed a rear view of girls in bikinis from the 70's and girls from 2000's what a difference. Girls don't seem to have a waistline any more but go straight down.

At seventeen years old and having had a leg operation, it left me with a limp, as one leg seemed a little longer than the other, and it caused damage to the tissue in my spine. A surgical belt was made for me at the hospital.

After several fittings at the hospital the belt was finally made. It was just like a liberty bodice (which children wore after the war to keep warm) with wide two inch metal strips inserted between the layers of material, from top to bottom. With a lace that was threaded all the way down the back of it, this was pulled tight to make it fit. It started below my bust and ended on my hips and I had to wear it for two years. It was such a job to put on. I know how the ladies felt in a previous century when they had to be laced into their dresses.

It was fortunate being so slim, but suppose it added inches to my waist as the metal strips made it thick and heavy too. When I tried to leave it off my body would go all limp. So it would have to be worn again for another week or so, for me to be upright as I had become dependent on it; but it worked. I walked very straight and it cured my limp.

I often wish it was still in the cupboard so when pain in my back occurs I could wear it. But having a modern stretchy belt, it's what I use instead and wear it when my back is painful.

Are belts making a come back? I notice there are some wonderful designs in the shops but with tops worn over trousers or skirts they can't be seen. There are loads of belts in my wardrobe but none of them seem to fit me any more – having grown around the waist line. I shall have to wear hipsters more with a loose belt dangling around the hips instead. I like a tie on a sweater too it seems to detract from the ever expanding waistline.

Chapter 13

SUN CREAM, OR SUN BURN?

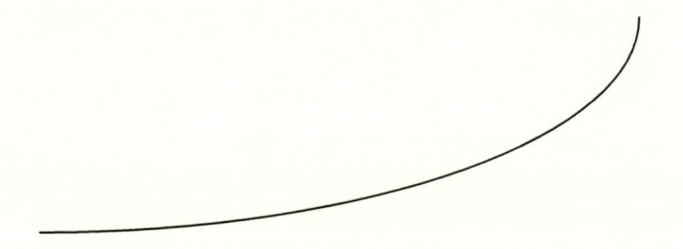

A long time ago my mother took my cousin Gillian and me for a day out at Hayling Island by coach, when we were about thirteen to fourteen years old. We went riding on the horses along the sand at a time before I had a phobia of horses. My mother got stung by a wasp or a bee and had her foot in a bandage, put on for her by the first aider on the beach. She was hobbling about all day but we sat out in the sun with my Nan telling us constantly not to get sunburned.

Another holiday we had down at Southend, further along the coast actually at Westcliffe on Sea in a guest house run by Nan's friends' daughter Mary. We were sitting on the beach with Nan and the sun was very hot. Nan kept telling Gill and me not to stay in the sun too long "you'll get sunburned" she would say; but at fourteen years old we didn't think it would matter. We were going to get a nice tan or so we thought.

What a shock we were in for that night. We couldn't sleep and kept poor old Nan up all night as we were in constant pain, burning up. Nan was putting cold compresses on our legs all through the night and we were glowing. It served us right, we should have listened to Nan, she knew best but at that age we thought we did.

I was reminded of this holiday and the burning sensation I had on my legs and the resulting scars from severe burn marks, when my beloved Mike and I went on holiday to Madeira. We were sitting by the pool and I kept telling Mike to cover himself up or put some sun cream on at least. No, he didn't need sun cream and he fell asleep.

That night did he suffer! He was so burnt we should in retrospect have gone to the hospital. His nipples had disappeared completely. His chest was so burnt and he was in agony. Putting cold flannels over his chest did nothing to ease his pain. The following day was the same and the following night.

Eventually he began to see his nipples again, what a relief. He has never taken his shirt off during the day on holiday again. It shook him rigid and he will remember the pain for a long, long time to come, as I did.

We always make sure the grandchildren are well covered, either with light clothing or plenty of sun cream. Julie and Caroline took their children to the beach on our holiday to Florida and were amazed at how much they had caught the sun as they didn't sunbathe. That's just the trouble you don't have to sunbathe especially when you are at the sea side, the breeze can cause the sun to burn. It all happens so quickly.

Once on a visit to Clacton with my mother, on a breezy, misty, overcast day. We had collapsible chairs with us and we sat talking on the beach nearly all day. Thinking of course that as the sun wasn't out, we wouldn't get sun burnt. How wrong can you be? We were burnt on our faces and my nose looked awful, all swollen and red and sore and the sun hadn't even shone through the clouds! But where my sunglasses had been there were huge white rings, my mother had the same. It gave us quite a laugh when we saw how ridiculous we both looked.

CHAPTER 14

MONTY versus TED

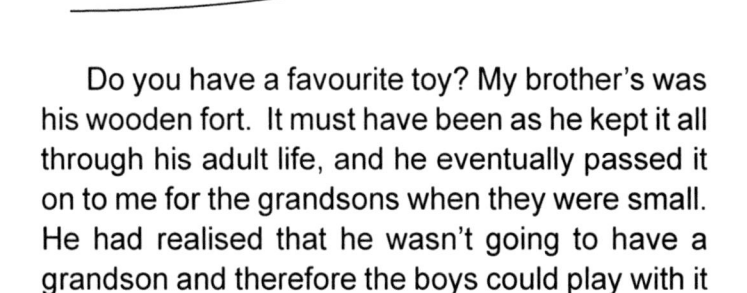

Do you have a favourite toy? My brother's was his wooden fort. It must have been as he kept it all through his adult life, and he eventually passed it on to me for the grandsons when they were small. He had realised that he wasn't going to have a grandson and therefore the boys could play with it when they came to visit.

I can see my brother now in our front room as a

boy lying on the floor with all his lead toy soldiers, some with cannons, some with rifles and others with back packs on. He would play for hours with them. He has passed a cannon on to me as well, which fires match sticks. It seems so small now.

My favourite was my Ted. My little Teddy who's hair I cut thinking it would grow, but of course it didn't. One day Monty our mongrel dog got hold of Ted and took him out into the garden. I saw him through the window at first with Ted in his mouth, shaking him as if he was trying to kill him. Poor Ted; I ran out into the garden and tried to get him off Monty. As I lunged towards Monty he darted to the side, then to the other side of me. He was obviously having a great time. At one point he put his two front paws together, growled with Ted in his mouth, dropped down onto his paws with his hind quarters in the air and his tail wagging. He was just looking me in the eye. I crouched down and lunged forward and almost caught Ted but Monty darted backwards; and I swear he was grinning at me.

He ran to the back of the garden and threw his head backwards, opened his mouth and rolled Ted further back into his mouth, then clenched his jaws on him again and ran towards me. I caught hold of Ted's leg and Monty started to snarl and shake his head, so we had a tug of war going on between us. This lasted for ages until I finally managed to get hold of poor; by now soggy, Ted.

His tummy was ripped open (no surprise there) so I lovingly took him upstairs, got a needle out of my sewing box and threaded it and proceeded to stitch him up. Monty came bounding up the stairs and I shooed him out of my room. Having sewn Ted's tummy and feeling quite pleased with it, I remember giving him such a hug.

Some weeks later my brother's Scout Troop were holding a jumble sale in their hall which was at the top of our road. I emptied my money out of my money box, about one shilling and six pence (approx seven and a half new pence) and walked to the Scout hut. As I went inside it seemed very dark, there were many long tables piled high with goods that people had brought for the Scouts to sell. I wandered around and bought one or two nick knacks, which left me with only three pence in my hand.

On my way out of the Scout hut I spotted a tiny wicker chair, a red and green arm chair, which would be just right for my Ted. I asked the Scout behind the table how much it was as there was no price on it, "three pence" he said, and as that's just what I had left, handed over the money and was delighted to bring the tiny chair home.

On returning home Ted was placed in his new arm chair, it fitted him perfectly and there he stayed for years, sitting upright and comfy; his arms resting on the arms of the chair. He was kept in the bottom of the airing cupboard as I grew older. There was no way he was going in the dustbin. He stayed there even when I was married.

The only clothes Ted owned was a tiny cardigan I had knitted, rolling the sleeves up so it fitted him. When we moved, again he sat in his chair; this time in one of the bedrooms which was to become one of my daughter's rooms.

When my first daughter Julie came along she was so tiny, I tried Ted's cardigan on her and it fitted. Having kept him for many years and all the years the girls were growing up, when Julie finally left home – she took my teddy with her. Still wearing his cardigan and sitting in his arm chair. He lives at her house now. He is almost bald and so small, but such a treasure. She tells me I gave him to her but I'm quite sure I didn't.

I asked her to let me see him the other day so I could take a photograph of him to put in this little book. He is so tiny and so ragged, poor little thing, fancy cutting off all his fur, I really thought when I was a child that it would grow again. His chair is broken now but he is still sitting in it.

Do you have memories of your favourite toy? They seemed so real at the time. It was just so lovely to talk to them and they kept quiet and didn't tell your secrets to anyone.

My cousin's daughter had an imaginary friend (a puppy) she would often be heard talking to it and of course there was no puppy there at all. She must have been a very lonely child or perhaps it was that she could say what she wanted without a come back from her friend!

My beloved Teddy

Chapter 15

CRIMPERS

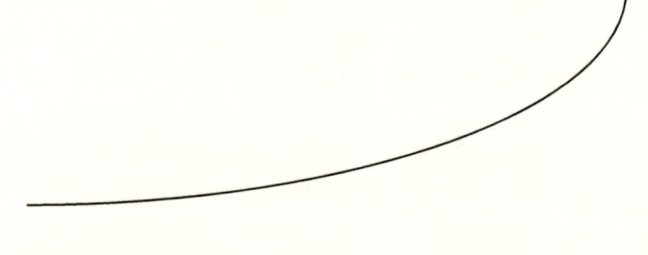

When I was very young my grandmother had an old battered pair of iron tongs. She told me that her mother used them to create a frill over an apron shoulder, and would crimp them all the way round, so they stood upright over the shoulder. She would place the tongs in hot coals from the open fire to warm them, and crimp them on a piece of paper or cloth, to check the temperature. Then she would proceed to crimp away until the whole frill had been bent into tiny wavy lines all the way round. She no doubt did this with collars as well.

Nan however, used them for curling hair, she would put them into hot water and leave them there for a short while, then with a piece of brown paper she would open them and close them with the paper in the middle, and if it burned the paper, then obviously they were too hot to curl the hair. Unfortunately for my cousin and me she often didn't wait for them to cool down properly; and we very often smelt the burning of hair being singed and our hair would come out in clumps. Poor Nan I don't think she ever meant for that to happen.

At about eight or nine years old my mother decided to perm my hair. She bought a home perm with a girl on the packet looking beautiful with gorgeous shiny hair, which is what I thought my hair was going to look like after it had been permed!

I was duly assigned to the bathroom and with a towel round my shoulders my mother proceeded to part my hair into sections, then into a pot she poured the pink lotion. Oh the smell of ammonia! It smelled the house out for days to come. Then she handed me a packet of tiny tissue papers (very much like my Granddad's cigarette papers only without the cardboard folder they came in) for me to hand to her, one every time she wanted to put another curler in my hair.

First she would take a piece of hair and soak it in the lotion, then fold a paper round it and proceed to curl it up until it reached my head, then close the fastener, until the whole head was covered. Then she soaked all the curlers and I was left with a towel round my neck and dripping curlers. I had to wait for what seemed hours before my hair was dry and she took the curlers out.

I was so looking forward to having curly hair after having straight hair for years. It was curly alright, so curly you couldn't brush it. I got the brush stuck in the curls and could not get it out. Getting very upset I began to cry. My hair looked awful and was put into bunches to hide the fact that it was now frizzy. I wasn't so keen to have a perm again the following year.

As we grew up it was metal curlers at first, flat ones with a flat slide and a square bar all the way round it, but it was so narrow that you couldn't get much hair in them.

Then plastic rollers came onto the market, much better and held in place with either a pin through the curler or a piece of elastic which stretched over the whole of the curler. Having washed the hair and put the curlers in place, a nylon cap or net was put over the whole head and you went to bed like that! Did we really do that?

I can remember when I had my long hair cut this was quite an experience for me, let alone what they must have looked like. The agony of the things pressing into your head was so uncomfortable and so unattractive.

At the hairdressers women would have rollers put all over their heads and a net placed over the whole lot; and then you sat under a hair dryer mounted either on the wall, or on a stand. The front lifted up for you to sit under it, then it was closed as you sat in your chair with your head inside the hood; and when you were comfortable a nylon cloth was placed over your shoulders. Then the hairdryer was switched on. Hot air would blow out over the curlers and onto your head until the hair was dry. It sometimes got very, very hot and your ears would burn.

When the hairdresser went to take the net off it would pull some of the rollers out and that hurt. What a process! And you would be red in the face too. And we paid for that experience!

Oh for heated rollers, what a boon they were in the sixties. They would straighten frizzy hair and curl straight hair. You just simply plugged them in and when the light went out they were at the right temperature. Then you put them in your hair, placed a pin over the whole curler and went on to the next one; and by the time your hair was all in curlers it was time to take the first one out.

These days it's heated hot brushes or 'curly wand' as I call them. When my little girl Julie was about three years old and going to a party, my wand was duly heated up and sat her on my lap, and thought I was going to make her look pretty by curling her hair.

Her hair was wound round the wand and was held there for the heat to penetrate. She started to cry, "What's the matter darling," I said. She wailed and wailed. It wasn't until I realised that I had actually held the wand across her ear, and was actually burning her ear that I took the wand away, only to see a very red, sore ear. Poor girl, no wonder she wanted long hair to wear in a pony tail after that. I never seemed to do this to Caroline and yet I also curled her hair with curling tongs.

Many a time rollers got stuck in my hair and after a lot of pulling and hair falling out in clumps, or even having to be cut out. I would be finally free of the wretched things. Oh for short straight hair these days.

Looking at photographs don't hair styles change! I can't believe that I have had such ridiculous styles in the past but I suppose at the time they didn't seems ridiculous - its how things change. I once had such short hair as a very young child, it was clipped at the back with stainless clippers and from that I went to having such long hair as a young woman I could almost sit on it. Then had it all cut off and wore it short again, what a mistake.

Chapter 16

MEMORIES

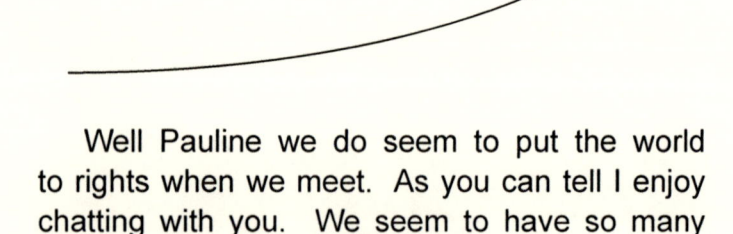

Well Pauline we do seem to put the world to rights when we meet. As you can tell I enjoy chatting with you. We seem to have so many memories that are so very similar.

Isn't an open log fire just wonderful to look at? Something you don't see so much of nowadays, but the mesmerising effect they have on you is amazing. The only thing is I feel it doesn't warm a room properly, especially if you have a dog. We had a dog that would always, always lie right in front of it when it was alight, so no one else could get near it. Consequently the back of the room was always much colder. Then the dog would get up and stand in front of it, if you pushed him away he would only come back again and promptly sit down so you couldn't even see it.

My mother once stood in front of the fire to get warm, and her new pleated skirt she had only put on a short while earlier, to go out somewhere special, caught light and was ruined. She was devastated and marched out of the room and changed into an old skirt. It's always the new things that get ruined – have you noticed?

We had our own chores to do in our house when I was little and one of my brothers many chores was to fetch the coal in, and light the fire. He used to scare me as he always put a sheet of newspaper across the front of the opening and the roar of the flames was awesome. Sometimes it would catch light and go up the chimney. Other times it would roar away beautifully for a few moments; then die down.

Then we moved on to an electric bar fire with the little spinning wheel balanced on a pin at the back, giving a glow effect to the fake coal at the bottom of the fire. These were very popular for a while in the fifties. My father made a panel to cover the whole of the fire place that looked like brick. The only thing was we still needed to light a coal fire to heat the water for a bath!

Then gas fires became popular. I never did like those. It could be that my mother was a nervous person; particularly where gas or electric was concerned. She always hated to light the gas fire as it always popped on igniting, and would whoosh so loudly.

So when we moved into our new home as a young married couple we had central heating. It never felt as comfortable as an open log fire, but the joy of coming in from the cold on a winter's night and just turning up the thermostat, and feel warmth coming out of the vents, was pure genius.

Radiators I have never liked. They are in the way and furniture can be placed in front of them, and so therefore you don't feel the heat as you should. Yes they are nice and warm to the touch but I don't feel they give out enough heat for a large room in winter, so I'll stick to my warm air heating, its instant. Perhaps I don't like change.

I do love to see the bonfire on firework night, there really is something magical about watching flames rise up in the air, and listening to it crackle.

My daughter Julie still has an open fire, although it is seldom used now as the flames would spit out a piece of burning wood, and the flooring would get burnt. If the logs were slightly damp it would sizzle and eject tiny red hot lumps onto the floor. They have central heating also but the fire place is central to the room, and long to see it lit, but sadly the log basket remains empty and the fire has candles in it for decoration only.

In my grandmother's day she had a fire place in all the rooms in her house, a large one in the main lounge and smaller ones in the bed rooms. It was the same in her bungalow at Henley, fireplaces in all the rooms which Granddad would light on a cold night.

When we first moved to Buckinghamshire we used to see the chimney sweep riding about on his bicycle, with his brushes on the back. He would be covered in soot, just like the coalman who wore a sack cloth over his head and shoulders that was black with the soot from the coal, something we don't see now.

There used to be an ice cream man who would have a large box on the front of his bicycle and he would lift the lid from the top to get an ice-lolly out. He always came round our street in the summer when we were children.

We also had an old rag and bone man who used to ride up and down our road when we were small children. He would call out "Rag Bone" and sit high up on his cart with a horse pulling it in front (usually with his head in a sack bag), and he had piles of old metal things on his cart and would collect iron and metal items that people no longer wanted.

We also had a milkman who had the old metal crates and what a noise they made early in the morning. You would hear him clunking his bottles and moving the crates about in his white Dairy van, you always knew what the time was when you heard him.

A man on a bicycle with a large wheel on the front would sharpen the knives and hedge cutters for a few pence. I used to stand and watch him work with the wheel spinning and him grinding something or other and watching the sparks flying out.

My brother and I used to lie on the floor in the dining room of an evening and listen to Dick Barton a children's programme on the radio, and be too scared to go upstairs to bed afterwards.

Then it was television. Do you remember your first television set? My Nan and Granddad had one that stood upright in a wooden cabinet with doors that closed when it was not in use, so it looked like a piece of furniture, not a TV set. We had one that stood on a table in the corner of the room but the screens were so small in those days. It almost seemed obscene to have a black square staring at you in the living room. I remember Muffin the mule with Annette Mills. As I grew up it was Six Five Special which I loved.

Oh I am getting all sentimental, it's amazing the things you forget, and yet with a sound or a smell, you can recall no end of memories. Even a piece of beaded fabric can have the same affect on me. I have a piece of beading that would have been used for a collar in my Great Grandmother's day, which my grandmother gave me.

My grandmother also gave me some very fine linen with broderie anglaise all round the bottom of the material. She told me that it was part of her mothers wedding underskirt. It pleased me to think the material her mother had given her had been kept wrapped up in tissue paper for years. When my first little girl Julie was tiny I made it into an angel top, with a gathered frill at the cuffs and the neck, which both she and Caroline wore. My grandmother was so pleased I had used the material and she thought the angel top was lovely.

I felt truly honoured to have been given it; and trusted that I would make something nice for my daughter out of it. I didn't understand why she hadn't used it, perhaps she had enough for what she wanted at the time and this was spare material.

My grandmother also made my cousin and me a camisole top out of broderie anglaise with a ribbon round it and gathered in at the waist. It made me feel so grown up wearing mine under a blouse, as it was so posh. No vest for me, but this very pretty and feminine top, with blue ribbon threaded through it.

Oh Pauline haven't I nattered on! It's so nice to talk when we meet after dropping Josh off for his golf lesson. See you next week and it will be your turn to chat (if I don't start all over again!).

Mike, Peter (my brother) me and Mother

About the Author

Doing 'lunch or coffee' with a friend or daughter and having a good old natter gives me such pleasure, as I feel life is passing me by so quickly. When looking at photographs of my mother or grandmother there is a lump in my throat as I can't talk to them anymore and wonder where have their lives gone? So friendships are especially valued.

I am so lucky to have both my daughters, six grandchildren and a wonderful husband and feel that I am truly blessed at last.